Where Is
Tennessee?

W0114247

Where Is Tennessee?

by Annette Whipple

illustrated by Ted Hammond

Penguin Workshop

To all readers who celebrate curiosity—AW

PENGUIN WORKSHOP
An imprint of Penguin Random House LLC
1745 Broadway, New York, NY 10019
penguinrandomhouse.com

Copyright © 2026 by Penguin Random House LLC

Penguin Random House values and supports copyright. Copyright fuels creativity, encourages diverse voices, promotes free speech, and creates a vibrant culture. Thank you for buying an authorized edition of this book and for complying with copyright laws by not reproducing, scanning, or distributing any part of it in any form without permission. You are supporting writers and allowing Penguin Random House to continue to publish books for every reader. Please note that no part of this book may be used or reproduced in any manner for the purpose of training artificial intelligence technologies or systems.

PENGUIN is a registered trademark and PENGUIN WORKSHOP is a trademark of Penguin Books Ltd. WHO HQ & Design is a registered trademark of Penguin Random House LLC.

Designed and Produced by Dinardo Design, LLC.

Library of Congress Cataloging-in-Publication Data is available.

First published in the United States of America by Penguin Workshop, 2026

Manufactured in the United States of America
CJKW

ISBN 9798217053438 (paperback)
10 9 8 7 6 5 4 3 2 1

ISBN 9798217053445 (library binding)
10 9 8 7 6 5 4 3 2 1

The authorized representative in the EU for product safety and compliance is Penguin Random House Ireland, Morrison Chambers, 32 Nassau Street, Dublin D02 YH68, Ireland, https://eu-contact.penguin.ie.

Contents

Where Is Tennessee?

Around two in the morning on December 16, 1811, people from Arkansas to New York City were shaken awake by an earthquake. In Tennessee, people heard noises such as thunder, screaming, and the cries of animals. The air smelled like rotten eggs while the quakes continued. As the morning sun lit the new day, another violent quake shook the ground.

The New Madrid earthquakes made the land rise and fall like ocean waves. They bent large trees and created ten-foot-wide cracks in the ground. Hundreds of earthquakes and aftershocks rocked the people of Tennessee during the winter of 1811–1812. The land of Tennessee was changed forever.

People had been building their homes on that

land for thousands of years. Those who lived through the New Madrid earthquakes had to be determined and creative. They repaired, rebuilt, and helped make Tennessee what it is today.

CHAPTER 1
Tennessee Land and First People

One of the most magnificent views in North America is Tennessee's Great Smoky Mountains. Smoke doesn't cover the mountains, though it looks that way. Plants and trees on the mountains give off vapors, which are a hazy fog or mist in the air. When the vapors combine with the air, we see the blue mist that has come to symbolize Tennessee. These mountains are part of the Appalachian Mountains, a range that stretches from Alabama all the way north into Canada. (The pronunciation of the word *Appalachian* varies from region to region, but many folks in Tennessee say appa-LATCH-un.)

The land of Tennessee includes the peaks and valleys of the Great Smoky Mountains, flat plains, and rolling hills. The area—and the life there—is diverse. With cool winters and warm summers, about two hundred kinds of trees cover more than half of Tennessee. Animals such as raccoons, American toads, and woodpeckers make their homes on land while catfish, beavers, and an occasional alligator swim through its streams, rivers, and lakes.

Tennessee is nearly four times as long as it is tall. The Great Smoky Mountains are on the eastern side, while the mighty Mississippi River forms the state's western border. Seven states surround Tennessee: Missouri, Mississippi, North Carolina, Arkansas, Kentucky, Virginia, and Georgia.

Underground, about ten thousand caves

and caverns form pockets deep into the land of Tennessee. That's more than any other state. Rushing water pours over Ruby Falls. At 260 feet high, this Chattanooga waterfall is underground! It is the tallest and deepest underground waterfall open to the public in the United States. The Lost Sea in Sweetwater, located between Knoxville and Chattanooga, is America's largest underground lake.

People have admired Tennessee's natural wonders for thousands of years. The first people to make Tennessee their home were hunters and gatherers. They used resources from the land and rivers for food and shelter. We don't know what these people called themselves, but they're known in history as the Woodland and Mississippian period peoples.

We do know that these prehistoric (prior to written history) people created art because we have some of it. Near Lebanon, Tennessee, a farmer found an 18.5-inch-tall carved sculpture of a kneeling man that dates from the Mississippian period. The stone sculpture was nicknamed Sandy. Today the McClung Museum

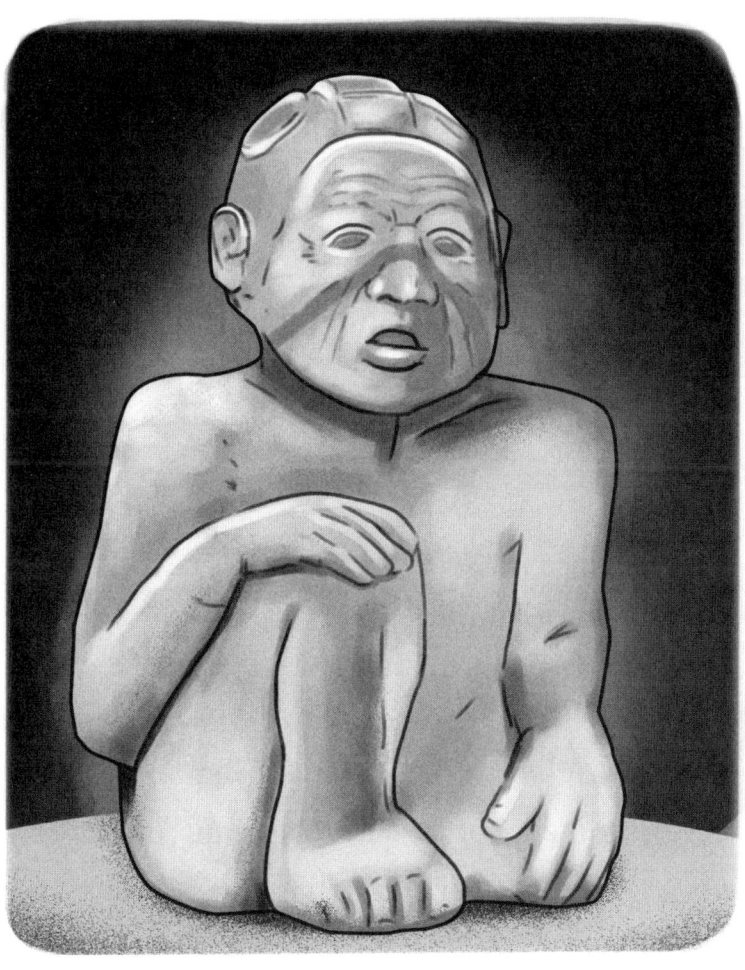

of Natural History and Culture at the University of Tennessee, Knoxville displays this sculpture, as well as other art and historical human-made items called artifacts.

As the Woodland and Mississippian period peoples began farming, they settled into villages, including in the Mississippi River Valley. They made art, like pottery, and developed their skills growing crops. Some of their villages created giant mounds as early as 300 BCE and as "recently" as 1350 CE. The mounds are so big, they may have taken as long as two hundred years to build.

Many, many people worked on each mound. They used stone tools and carried soil in baskets or animal skins. Evidence of fifty mounds have been found at the Pinson Mounds, Mound Bottom, and Castalian Spring Mounds, spread over three hundred miles of Tennessee. Even though the mounds likely got smaller over time, today one of the Pinson Mounds still stands seventy-two feet high! That's as tall as a seven-story building. The mounds often had structures on top of them which were part of the communities. Some were religious centers, burial sites, or even homes.

Eventually, the descendants of the Woodland and Mississippian period peoples formed groups. The Chickasaw (say: CHICK-uh-saw) Nation settled in the western part of the land we now call Tennessee. In the east, the Cherokee (say: CHAIR-oh-kee) Nation settled. They called their home *Shaconage* which means "place of the blue smoke." Shawnee, Creek, and other nations also lived in what is now Tennessee. The state's name comes from a Cherokee village called Tanasi.

In 1540, the Spanish explorer Hernando de Soto, along with hundreds of soldiers, servants, and enslaved people, reached what would become Tennessee. The group looked for gold, silver, copper, and river pearls. They hunted and gathered food to eat and traded with Indigenous groups for items such as mulberries and honey. This was before there were honeybees in North America, so Indigenous people likely received the honey from trading with the Mayan people, in what is now Central America.

More groups from Spain, France, and England came looking for riches. They built forts and claimed land for their countries. European contact led to hardship for the Cherokee and Chickasaw Nations, as well as other Indigenous groups.

Many Indigenous people died from diseases like smallpox, which they had never been exposed to before. Others fought with settlers over resources. The French killed many from the Natchez Nation when they were at war. Shawnee people were forced to move by settlers who wanted their land. Europeans enslaved some Indigenous people. Some Indigenous groups became part of larger nations.

In 1763, the British (also called English)

government made a law that all land between the Atlantic Ocean and the Appalachian Mountains was for European settlers. The land in the west was reserved for Indigenous nations. But in just five years, the treaty called the Proclamation of 1763 was broken and European settlers moved west to what would become Tennessee.

Though Indigenous, French, and Spanish people explored, hunted, and trapped on the land of Tennessee at different times, the British now dominated. In 1775, the war called the American Revolution began between the thirteen colonies and the British. The colonies won their independence to become the United States of America.

Tennessee wasn't a state yet. Few settlers lived there. In 1784, a few counties banded together and called themselves the state of Franklin. It had its own governor—but the United States thought it was too far west.

Wilderness Road

Daniel Boone blazed—or created—the first trail from Tennessee to Kentucky. He knew more about the local land and trails than other white settlers. Investors hired Boone to create a road so more settlers could move west of the Appalachian Mountains.

In 1775, Boone led about thirty men out of what is now called Kingsport, Tennessee. They chopped down trees and brush to make a new trail. It went through the Appalachian Mountains in a place called the Cumberland Gap, where Kentucky, Virginia, and Tennessee now meet. Though called the Wilderness Road, it was really a rough trail that often had to be traveled on foot.

At first the Wilderness Road was about two hundred miles in length. Then it became even longer. By 1792, the road stretched to Knoxville,

Tennessee. An estimated three hundred thousand settlers traveled the Wilderness Road between 1775 and 1810.

On June 1, 1796, the United States finally admitted Tennessee as the sixteenth state. Knoxville was the capital where government decisions were made. Soon, the capital's location would change.

CHAPTER 2
Early Tennessee

Early on, most settlers in Tennessee farmed. They grew corn and raised hogs for their own food. They made yarn and fabric for clothes. They used animal hides to make saddles and shoes. They built their own furniture and tools. Some farms sold tobacco and cotton. Some communities had a gristmill to grind grain into flour and a blacksmith who made things with iron—like nails and horseshoes. As communities grew, towns became more important.

Industry, made up of businesses that provided products and services, grew alongside agriculture. Many shop owners used local sources to make and sell products. After cotton and wool were cleaned and prepared in mills, other businesses bought the woven cloth, then sold it themselves.

Many farmers in Tennessee were enslavers at the time. The farmers purchased people who had been kidnapped from Africa and brought to North America or their descendants. Since the government considered enslaved people the owner's property, they were forced to work for no pay. As most businesses relied on local farms for raw materials, they relied on slavery, too.

Though many communities grew, they also faced setbacks. During the winter of 1811–1812, thousands of earthquakes shook Tennessee for months. Some were huge earthquakes that were felt as far away as Canada and Boston. They were the worst earthquakes in American history up to that point and are still some of the worst. Landslides and water destroyed settlements along the Mississippi River. Riverbanks washed away.

Reelfoot Lake formed. The tremors made some river islands disappear. New hills and valleys formed. Waves crashed over the Mississippi River's banks. The earthquakes even caused the river to flow upstream temporarily. It ran backward! The New Madrid earthquakes were named after a town that they destroyed. They are remembered because they changed the land forever.

Months after the earthquakes, the Tennessee governor asked for 3,500 volunteers to fight the British in what became the War of 1812. By the time the war ended in 1815, about 28,000 Tennessee men signed up to fight the British along with General Andrew Jackson. That was nearly ten times more than asked for! Though there was no clear winner, national pride increased in the United States as it became more independent from England. And with so many men going to fight, Tennessee earned a new nickname: the Volunteer State.

Throughout Tennessee, towns continued to form. One unique community was Free Hill. Virginia Hill was a white woman whose family were enslavers. She decided to end this enslavement and bought land near the Tennessee-Kentucky border. She gave these freed people the land while slavery was still legal. The new residents made the land a successful town, despite facing challenges. The land wasn't ideal for farming,

and there were threats from white outsiders. Yet Free Hill thrived with about three hundred residents. This Black community included stores, social clubs, churches, and restaurants, as well as a school for children. Some descendants of the original residents still live there today.

Indigenous people also lived throughout the state, like Nancy Reece. She was Cherokee and lived in Chattanooga until she was sent away to a school called Brainerd Mission. In the 1800s, US politicians forced Indigenous children to attend government boarding schools, taking them away from their families. These schools made Indigenous children act, speak, and dress like white Americans. Students couldn't speak their native languages and were often abused. At Brainerd, Reece learned English and about Christianity. Eventually, she got married and returned to Chattanooga. She and her husband couldn't stay for long.

The US government wanted to make more room for white settlers in Tennessee. President Andrew Jackson passed a law in 1830 that forced Indigenous people to move west of the Mississippi River. It was called the Indian Removal Act. At first, most Indigenous people stayed. The US Army forced them to leave. Reece and her husband were among the thousands of people who were removed from Tennessee.

In 1838, about seven thousand US soldiers on horseback began marching groups of men, women, and children away from their homes. Most were from the Cherokee Nation like Reece. Some were from the Chickasaw, Creek, and other Indigenous nations.

The marching people endured harsh weather, hunger, and lack of clothing. The Choctaw Nation marched without food or supplies. Thousands died. Survivors were forced to keep walking, even though they were mourning. After

walking fifteen miles in one day, Reece gave birth
to her first baby. The next day, she was forced to
march more than ten miles.

The group walked hundreds of miles to what
is now Oklahoma. Reece, her husband, Joseph
Starr, and their baby son, Jug, were some of the
Indigenous people who had to start again in
Oklahoma. We now call this forced march and

the path they took the Trail of Tears.

The Tennessee government was making decisions, too. During the early 1800s, Tennessee's capital didn't stay in Knoxville. It moved to Kingston—but only for a day. Later it moved to Nashville and Murfreesboro as the state's population grew. In 1843, the capital returned to Nashville permanently.

In 1861, the Civil War divided the nation and the people of Tennessee. The Union (Northern states) supported ending slavery, and the Confederacy (Southern states) wanted slavery to continue. Whether Tennessee would secede—or leave—the United States and join the Confederacy was put to a vote. The majority of the people chose to remain with the Union. Soon, the people of Tennessee thought the Union army was too harsh and changed their minds. After another vote, Tennessee joined the Confederacy.

Many men from Tennessee joined the army and trained as Confederate soldiers. In East Tennessee, many people still supported the Union. Eventually, thirty-one thousand Tennessee men joined the Union troops.

Tennessee prepared to fight the Union armies by building forts. Before they were finished, the state was taken over by Union soldiers. The North controlled the rivers and took over

Nashville. The battles left Tennessee in shambles. Union soldiers sometimes destroyed buildings and killed livestock. The law wasn't functioning and couldn't help. Local gangs were part of the violence. Schools and churches couldn't operate. Even newspapers shut down. Violence, death, and hunger ruled the land.

In some towns, the Union helped restore schools, churches, and stores. But in rural areas, trouble continued. Traveling was dangerous.

The Civil War ended in 1865. Slavery was abolished, or outlawed. Tennessee was the first Confederate state to meet the requirements to become part of the United States again in 1866. It was time to move forward.

CHAPTER 3
Tennessee Grows

Though part of the United States again, Tennessee was in ruins following the Civil War. Reconstruction, a period of rebuilding, could finally begin. In addition to repairing businesses, homes, and farms, attitudes and relationships needed to change.

Tennessee was home to former Union and Confederate soldiers. They often returned to their communities to find their homes, land, animals, and food supplies in poor condition. Many plantation owners began renting out their land in a system called sharecropping. Rather than receiving wages, sharecroppers rented and worked small plots of land. In return, they would give a portion of the crops they produced to the landowner after the harvest. Because they had to rent tools and other supplies from the landowners, sharecroppers often ended up owing more than they earned. It was a system that benefited the plantation owners, who often treated sharecroppers very poorly.

Slavery was no longer legal, but challenges for Black people continued. During Reconstruction, a group of Confederate veterans formed the Ku Klux Klan (also called the KKK) in Pulaski, Tennessee, in 1866. This group of white men used violence and intimidation against Black people and those who supported freedom and equal rights. As the Ku Klux Klan spread throughout the state and the country, so did racist violence. Black men, women, and children were terrorized and killed. Despite threats, some white people stood up for the rights of Black people.

The Black historian and educator W. E. B. Du Bois (say: doo-BOYS) had attended Fisk

University in Nashville and was a teacher in rural Tennessee. He became famous for promoting equal rights for all people. Ida B. Wells was another well-known civil rights activist in the late 1800s. She was enslaved as a girl. After the war, she taught school in Memphis and cared for

her siblings. She wrote for newspapers under the pen name of Iola. She used a fake name because her articles on topics like segregation (separation based on the color of skin) and violence against Black people made her a target. Many people didn't want these truths discussed. The work of Du Bois, Wells, and many others began to create change.

Even with these challenges, industry in Tennessee increased. The cities of Knoxville and Chattanooga boomed. Furniture, sawmill, gristmill, and ironwork businesses grew. Farming was still important, but now there were more ways to make a living.

New times meant new entertainment. In the 1860s, Black musicians performed on Beale Street in Memphis near busy shops and restaurants. A millionaire named Robert Church built a social center and first-class hotel for Black people there. Beale Street was alive with music all day and night. Later, legendary musicians like trumpeter Louis Armstrong and singer Ella Fitzgerald would sing about Beale Street and its importance.

In the early 1900s, Black musicians often combined the sounds of their past. They grew up singing church hymns and blended that with the rhythm of African music and spirituals which had been passed down by enslaved and free people for generations. They used these influences and others to create a new, uniquely American style of music called the blues. Musicians like Memphis Minnie sang blues music with great emotion.

When the Great Depression hit the United States in 1929, people didn't have spare money for entertainment. Many businesses and factories couldn't pay their employees, and people lost their jobs. When banks across the state closed, many people lost all their savings. Families struggled to pay their bills and buy food. Clothing was repaired again and again, and some was sewn

Memphis Minnie performing

from flour bags. People were hungry. Charities couldn't keep up with the needs of communities, and people suffered.

Tennessee—and six other states—had help from a national program called the Tennessee Valley Authority (TVA). Beginning in 1933, the TVA hired people for projects that would provide jobs and make communities better. It built dams that controlled flooding and created electricity. It helped farmers and business owners. It developed agriculture and industry. It even helped establish the Great Smoky Mountains as a national park!

Slowly, regular employment returned to Tennessee. Since people had jobs again, they also wanted to be entertained. And Tennessee knew how to do that with music. In the mid-1950s, Memphis became known as the birthplace of rock and roll, a new kind of music with a strong beat and electric instruments. Elvis Presley was famous across the nation and around the world and is still called the King of Rock and Roll. Fans adored him, and he inspired other musicians for decades. Gospel singer Mahalia Jackson became a legend in Memphis and around the world. A radio variety show called the Grand Ole Opry in Nashville began focusing on country music in 1925. It made people like Hank Williams and Dolly Parton famous. Musician Bertha Bearden Dorsey went by the name Ruby Falls (named after the landmark) and became a well-known country star in the 1970s.

Black and white people couldn't attend concerts together in many parts of the United States as segregation continued. Racist ideas and laws were still a problem in Tennessee and throughout the nation. In the 1950s, the civil rights movement strengthened. Many people supported equal rights for all people and ending segregation. Many still showed their disagreement in hateful and violent ways.

People worked to get laws passed that would allow children to attend schools that weren't segregated by race. These civil rights workers wanted all people to be treated with respect. They didn't think tests should be given to "allow" a person to vote. But change was slow.

In Clinton, Tennessee, Black high school students had to ride a bus twenty miles to attend an all-Black school. They couldn't attend their local school because of segregation. In 1956, a

law was passed that allowed Black students to attend schools in town. Many white people didn't like the decision.

Twelve Black students signed up to attend school in Clinton. These students, called the Clinton 12, faced angry mobs at school. The Ku Klux Klan tried to intimidate them. The school had to close because of the violence. The National Guard was called in to protect the Clinton 12. Six of the twelve students finished the year at Clinton High School, and two of the original

twelve students went on to graduate from the school.

Local pastors (church leaders) like James Lawson and Kelly Miller Smith worked as leaders in the civil rights movement in Tennessee. They led the way, encouraging justice and equality without violence. In 1968, another pastor named Dr. Martin Luther King Jr. visited Memphis to help protest low pay for sanitation workers (people who help dispose of a city's garbage), most of whom were Black. It was in Memphis that Dr. King was killed because of his work. His death was a tragedy. But leaders of the movement still hoped to improve life for the Black community in Tennessee and throughout the United States.

Even as it struggled with racial violence and civil rights issues, the state's industries boomed. Tennessee became known for making clothing and technology, including energy products such as natural gas, oil, and electricity. Nissan, General

Motors, and other car companies opened factories in the state. Colleges were built to educate the growing population.

With all of its growth and changes, Tennessee invited the world to visit when it hosted the 1982 World's Fair. A giant golden ball called the Sunsphere, which can still be seen today, greeted visitors to Knoxville as they arrived. Countries from around the world displayed their newest technology and other national achievements. By hosting, Knoxville showcased and preserved history—including their own energy industry.

CHAPTER 4
Tennessee Today

Long-standing traditions, as well as changes, still shape Tennessee. Agriculture continues with crops like cotton, soybeans, and tobacco. The booming dairy industry has helped make milk the state drink. Tennessee Walking Horses (a famous breed known for their running walk and gentleness) were founded in the state. Shelbyville

hosts one of the largest horse shows in the world to celebrate Walking Horses.

Local trees are harvested for lumber and wood products. Tennessee ranks third in the nation for making hardwood lumber. Crushed stone and gravel are collected and sold for construction purposes. Copper and silver are mined as well as large amounts of coal.

Technology continues to be important. Computers, electronics, and cars from General Motors, Nissan, Toyota, and Volkswagen are produced in Tennessee. The state makes a new car every twenty seconds! Mountain Dew soda, MoonPie sweets (made of chocolate, graham crackers, and marshmallows), cotton candy (originally called fairy floss), and Goo Goo Clusters (made of caramel, marshmallow nougat, peanuts, and chocolate) all had their start in Tennessee.

Nashville is still the heart of country music.

The Grand Ole Opry has featured musicians for more than one hundred years. It's also the home of Country Music Association's annual music festival. Superstar and country music legend Dolly Parton promotes Appalachian culture at her Dollywood theme park and resort to about four million tourists a year in the small town of

Pigeon Forge. Visitors can explore this town in the Smoky Mountains with shows, shopping, and extreme adventures. Elvis Presley's Memphis mansion and entertainment complex, called Graceland, is dedicated to his life and career. It is the most visited home in the country other than the White House.

Dolly Parton (1946—)

Dolly Parton was born into a family with twelve children. Her parents were East Tennessee sharecroppers. They didn't have much, but they had music. By the time Dolly was ten years old, she was performing on radio and television shows.

Before she graduated from high school, she was an experienced songwriter.

Though Dolly's roots were in country music, she recorded hit albums for pop music fans, too. She starred in television and movies and became famous throughout the world. But Dolly's heart was always in Tennessee. She wanted her beloved Great Smoky Mountains to be enjoyed by all and knew a theme park would bring visitors to the land she loved. Today, her park is known as Dollywood.

Dolly's father inspired her. He was smart and hardworking, but he could not read. Dolly knew others were like him, and she created a program to send free books to children. It began in Tennessee, but now young children around the world benefit from Dolly Parton's Imagination Library.

Car racing fans can visit the Bristol Motor Speedway, while history buffs appreciate many Civil War sites and museums. The Parthenon museum in Nashville surprises visitors because it is an exact-size replica of the Parthenon found in Athens, Greece. At the Sequoyah Birthplace Museum in Vonore, visitors learn about Sequoyah. Raised by his mother, Wuh-teh of the Paint clan in Tennessee, Sequoyah developed a written version of the spoken Cherokee language in the early 1800s. The museum also has walking trails. Serious hikers can walk about two hundred miles along the Tennessee and North Carolina border on the Appalachian Trail. This trail stretches from Georgia all the way to Maine. Some people hike portions of it while others hike the entire trail.

Tennessee's cities and small towns have a lot to offer. People flock to the Great Smoky Mountains National Park with its incredible mountain and valley views. This part of the Appalachian

Mountains, with more than eight hundred miles of hiking trails, draws more visitors than any other national park. Visitors from around the world appreciate the wide diversity of wildlife—including the unique synchronous fireflies that flash their lights at the same time.

Challenging times come to Tennessee, too. On September 27, 2024, Hurricane Helene struck East Tennessee. Homes, businesses, schools, and more were destroyed by wind, rain, and flooding. Farm crops, roads, and bridges were washed away. The hurricane devastated Tennessee, but communities are cleaning up and working hard to repair and rebuild.

With natural beauty, vibrant culture, and rich history, it's no wonder more than seven million people call Tennessee home. The people of Tennessee have a long history of determination and creativity, and the state offers a unique charm found nowhere else!

Tennessee at a Glance

Statehood: 1796

Nickname: The Volunteer State

Abbreviation: TN

State Motto: Agriculture and Commerce

Nashville

State Tree: Tulip poplar

State Animal: Raccoon

Capital: Nashville

Size: 42,144 square miles

Population: Over 7 million

Famous People from Tennessee: Kenny Chesney (musician), Davy Crockett (folk hero and politician), Morgan Freeman (actor), Tina Turner (musician), Wilma Rudolph (Olympic athlete)

State flag

State flower
Iris

State bird
Mockingbird

FUN FACT:

In 1971, fossils including a nine-inch fang of a saber-toothed cat were found in Nashville. Today, the city's professional hockey team, the Nashville Predators, has some of the bones on display at their arena.

Timeline of Tennessee

300 BCE	The Woodland period people live in Tennessee
900 CE	The Mississippian period people live in Tennessee
1540	Hernando de Soto searches for riches in Tennessee
1763	The Proclamation of 1763 bans European settlers from living west of the Appalachian Mountains
1775	Daniel Boone's team creates the Wilderness Road through the Cumberland Gap
1796	Tennessee becomes the sixteenth state
1811	Hundreds of earthquakes shake Tennessee, creating the illusion that the Mississippi River is flowing upriver
1830	The Indian Removal Act forces the removal of eastern Indigenous people to west of the Mississippi
1861	Tennessee joins the Confederate States of America
1866	Tennessee rejoins the United States
1909	Blues music style becomes popular in Memphis
1925	The Grand Ole Opry begins as a radio variety show
1968	Dr. Martin Luther King Jr. is killed in Memphis
1982	Knoxville hosts the World's Fair
1986	Dollywood opens near Pigeon Forge
2024	Hurricane Helene devastates East Tennessee

Timeline of the World

312 BCE — The first great road in Rome is built

1607 CE — Jamestown, the first permanent English settlement, is founded

1821 — Panama, Guatemala, and Santo Domingo gain independence from Spain

1876 — Alexander Graham Bell places the world's first telephone call

1914 — The Panama Canal officially opens, connecting the Atlantic and Pacific Oceans

1928 — Penicillin is discovered

1946 — The first electronic computer is built

1969 — Neil Armstrong is the first person to walk on the moon

1992 — The World Wide Web becomes available to the public

1994 — Nelson Mandela becomes president of South Africa

2023 — India passes China as the country with the most people in the world

2024 — About 15,000 athletes compete in the Summer Olympics and Paralympics hosted in Paris, France

Bibliography

*Books for young readers

Deter-Wolf, Aaron, and Tanya M. Peres. *Mastodons to Mississippians: Adventures in Nashville's Deep Past*. Nashville: Vanderbilt University Press, 2021.

*Edgers, Geoff. *Who Was Elvis Presley?* New York: Penguin Workshop, 2007.

*Kelley, True. *Who Is Dolly Parton?* New York: Penguin Workshop, 2014.

*Kramer, S. A. *Who Was Daniel Boone?* New York: Penguin Workshop, 2006.

*McDaniel, Melissa. *Tennessee: My United States*. New York: Children's Press, 2018.

*Smith, Sherri L. *What Is the Civil Rights Movement?* New York: Penguin Workshop, 2020.

"Tennessee." *Britannica*. https://www.britannica.com/place/Tennessee.

Websites

The Tennessee Encyclopedia of History and Culture: tennesseeencyclopedia.net

The Tennessee Historical Society: tennesseehistory.org

Tennessee History for Kids: www.tnhistoryforkids.org

Tennessee State Museum: tnmuseum.org